CHI

ACPL ITEM
DISCARDED

P9-CSE-974

Metal

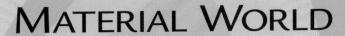
Metal

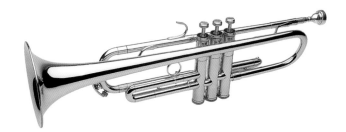

by Claire Llewellyn

FRANKLIN WATTS
A Division of Scholastic Inc.
NEW YORK TORONTO LONDON AUCKLAND SYDNEY
MEXICO CITY NEW DELHI HONG KONG
DANBURY, CONNECTICUT

First published in 2002 by
Franklin Watts
96 Leonard Street
London EC2A 4XD

First American edition 2002 by Franklin Watts
A Division of Scholastic Inc.
90 Sherman Turnpike
Danbury, CT 06816

Text copyright © Claire Llewellyn 2002

ISBN 0-531-14632-4 (lib. bdg.) 0-531-14834-3 (pbk.)

Catalog details are available from the
Library of Congress Cataloging-in-Publication data

Series Editor: Rosalind Beckman
Series Designer: James Evans
Picture Research: Diana Morris
Photography: Steve Shott

Printed in Hong Kong, China

Acknowledgments

Thanks are due to the following for kind permission to
reproduce photographs:

AKG London: 7cl. Klaus Andrews/Still Pictures: 9t. Mark
Andrews/Still Pictures: 9c. Austrian Archives/Corbis: 16b. Yann
Arthus-Betrand/Corbis: 26c. Boodles & Dunthorne: 16cr. BSIP,
Boucharlat/SPL: 13t. John Cancalosi/Still Pictures: 18c. Christies
Images/Corbis: 20b. James Davis Travel Photography: 8b. Chris
Fairclough/Franklin Watts: 25b. Favre Felix/Jerrican/ SPL: 22b
Dylan Garcia/Still Pictures: 24b. Ron Giling/Still Pictures: 18b.
Gunshots/The Art Archive: 12t, 12b. Ben Johnson/SPL: 26b.
Damien Lovegrove/SPL: 27c. John Mead/SPL: 27t. Ray
Moller/Franklin Watts: 15t. Dagli Orti/Historical Museum
Sofia/The Art Archive: 16t. Vittoriano Rastelli/Corbis: 10b.
Rosenfeld Images Ltd/SPL: 23c. Charles E Rotkin/Corbis: b
cover. Horst Scafer/Still Pictures: 25t. Paul Seheult/Eye
Ubiquitous: 21t. Heine Schneebelj/SPL: 19t. Kaj R Svensson/
SPL: 18t. Hugh Turvey/SPL: 7br. Nick Wiseman/Eye
Ubiquitous: 17t. Dove Wren/Eye Ubiquitous: 23t.

Thanks are also due to John Lewis for their help
with this book.

Contents

Words printed in **bold italic** are explained in the glossary.

What Is Metal?

Metal is one of the world's most useful materials. Look around and you will see that we use metal everywhere. We use it in our cars, offices, homes, and schools. It is hard to imagine life without metal.

All Sorts of Metals

There are more than eighty different kinds of metal. One metal can look and feel a little different from another. It might be used in a different way.

Made of Metal

All the things in these pictures are made of metal. Can you name them all? What do they feel like?

Material Words

Which of these words describes metal?

cold   thick   shiny

sticky   stretchy

stiff   solid

heavy

soft   strong

dull

hard

warm

durable

spongy   light

crisp

colorful

rough   smooth

thin

flexible   slimy

springy

squashy

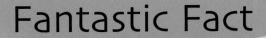

Fantastic Fact

Most metals are solid, but one is liquid. It is called mercury, and it is used in thermometers.

Metal Is Hard and Strong

Many metals are hard and strong. They can stand up to very heavy wear. That is why metal is used to make buildings, machines, and cars.

Standing Strong

Most big buildings have a framework made of metal beams. The metal framework holds up the building and stops it from falling down. Many bridges hang from metal cables or are made of metal beams.

The Golden Gate bridge in San Francisco hangs from strong metal cables that run down into the ground.

Working Hard

Think of all the machines that are made of metal: washing machines, cars, drills, cranes, and more. All these machines have moving parts. Metal is the only material that could take such wear and tear.

Factory and farming machines need to be strong because they are used for heavy work. They are mostly made of metal.

Try This

Eat a little bit of spinach or watercress and you are eating a metal called iron. Many foods contain tiny bits of metal. They are very good for the body and help keep you strong.

watercress

spinach

Metal is smooth and shiny

Most metal is smooth, easy to clean, and very shiny. If you do not clean them, some metals lose their shine. They become dull or even **rusty**.

Keeping Clean

In large kitchens where hundreds of meals are cooked every day, there is lots of metal equipment. This is because metal is durable and easy to keep clean. At home, kitchen sinks and taps are often made of metal, too.

Restaurant kitchens need to be free of germs. Metal tools and worktops are easy to clean.

Staying Shiny

Silver cutlery and candlesticks look beautiful when they are polished. After a while, the metal gets dull and needs cleaning again. Some metals need extra care if they are outside because the damp air makes them get rusty.

Silver candlesticks only stay shiny if they are cleaned regularly.

These garden shears are going rusty. They need to be cleaned and oiled.

Try This

Find a dirty metal object such as an old spoon or coin, and polish it with a cloth and some metal cleaner. What happens to the object? What happens to the cloth?

11

Metal Can Be Very Sharp

Metal is so hard that if you rub it with a stone, it becomes very sharp. Metal has been used to make tools and weapons for many thousands of years.

Metal Weapons

When people discovered metal about eight thousand years ago, they used it to make weapons. Metal spearheads, swords, and axes were sharp and strong. They were better for hunting and fighting than weapons made of wood or stone.

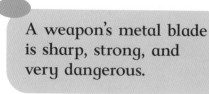

A weapon's metal blade is sharp, strong, and very dangerous.

Metal Tools

Many tools have a sharp metal blade that is used to cut other materials. Saws, axes, scissors, and knives are part of our everyday lives. They are used in hospitals, restaurants, forests, and farms.

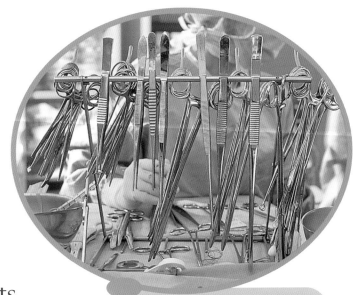

Sharp metal tools are used by doctors in the operating theatre.

WARNING

Always be careful with sharp tools. They can easily cut you.

Try This

Find two shovels, one made of metal and the other made of plastic. Try digging with them. Is there any difference between them?

Metal Carries Heat and Electricity

Materials that allow heat or **electricity** to pass through them are called **conductors**. Metal is a very useful material because it conducts both heat and electricity.

Carrying Heat

Metal allows heat to pass through it quickly. If you put a metal saucepan over a flame, it heats up and starts to cook the food. Many hot machines, such as ovens and irons, are also made of metal.

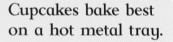

Cupcakes bake best on a hot metal tray.

Most metal saucepans have a wooden or plastic handle. A metal handle would heat up very quickly and be uncomfortable to hold.

Carrying Electricity

Electricity is carried along metal wires from power stations to our homes. Electricity can be dangerous, so the wires are wrapped inside plastic cords. Plastic does not conduct electricity, so it keeps people safe.

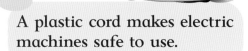

A plastic cord makes electric machines safe to use.

This piece of plastic cord has been cut away to show the metal wires inside.

Inside a light bulb is a thin metal thread. When electricity flows across the metal, the thread glows and gives out light.

Try This

Take two metal spoons. Put one in a mug of cold water and the other in a mug of very warm water. Leave them to stand for a few minutes. Now take them out, dry them, and feel them. What do you notice?

Some Metals Are Precious

Some metals, such as gold, silver, and **platinum**, are not easily found. They are called precious metals, and they are used to make special things.

gold necklace worn by a Roman over two thousand years ago

Rare Metals

gold and cameo bracelet

Metals such as iron are very common and are used to make many things. Other metals are more rare. Gold and platinum are the most precious metals. They have a beautiful color and shine.

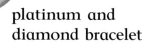

platinum and diamond bracelet

white gold and diamond necklace

gold earrings

Precious Goods

People have always prized precious metals and used them to make jewelry and other beautiful things. Gold and silver were used to make the first coins because they showed the value of the money. Today's coins are made from much cheaper metals.

Churches are special buildings. The roof of this Russian church has been covered with gold to make it look beautiful.

These coins are about five hundred years old. Can you see when the largest one was made?

Fantastic Fact

The front of an astronaut's helmet has a fine coating of gold. When bright sunlight hits the gold, it bounces back off again. This protects the astronaut's eyes from being damaged by the Sun.

Metal Is Dug Out of the Ground

A few metals are found in lumps called **nuggets**, but most are found inside rocks. The rocks have to be dug up and heated before the metal can be used.

Nuggets of gold (left) and *copper* (top). Only gold, silver, platinum, and copper are found as nuggets.

Digging Up Ores

Most metals are hidden inside rocks called **ores** and have to be dug out of the ground. This is sometimes done in open **quarries**, but more often in underground mines. Mining is hard, dirty, dangerous work. It can cost human lives.

This worker is mining for copper. His powerful drill is able to reach the metal ore deep inside the rock.

It takes the heat of a huge furnace to get the metal out of an ore.

Treating the Ores

To get the metal out of the rock, the ore must be crushed and heated in a *furnace*. The metal then melts and is poured away. As it cools, it turns hard again and can be used to make many things.

Fantastic Fact

The deepest mine in the world is a gold mine in South Africa. Miners have to work 2.5 miles (4 km) underground.

Metals Can Be Mixed Together

Metals can often be made better or stronger by mixing two of them together. The new mixture is called an **alloy**.

From Copper to Bronze

Copper was one of the first metals ever used by people. It was soft and easy to hammer. In time, people discovered that if they heated the copper and mixed it with a metal called tin, it made a much harder metal for weapons and tools. The new metal was called bronze.

Copper is a reddish-brown metal. Today, we use it to make the wires that carry electricity. It also makes the best pots and pans.

Since ancient times bronze has been used to make statues and sculptures such as this African mask.

Stainless Steel

Steel is a very strong metal made from iron. Steel rusts in the open air. When it is mixed with other metals, though, it produces an alloy called *stainless steel.* Stainless steel is very useful. It is used to make many things because it is strong and does not rust.

Kitchen tools are often made of stainless steel. They do not rust, even though they are always getting wet.

Try This

Find some nails made of iron or steel. Put a few in a dry jar and a few in a jar half filled with water. Seal both jars with a lid. Leave the jars for two weeks, then examine the nails. What do you find?

Metal Is Easy to Shape

If metal is heated until it softens or melts, it can be shaped into many different things. Shaping is usually done by factory machines.

Into a Mold

Metal melts when it is heated and hardens when it cools. While it is soft, it can be shaped in many different ways. Metal can be poured into a *mold* and left to cool until it sets into a solid shape.

Red-hot metal is poured into a mold. It is being made into a bell.

Pressing and Squeezing

Hot metal can be flattened by heavy rollers to make beams, sheets, and rails. It can be squeezed through small holes to make thin rods or wire. It can also be pressed into different shapes, such as the doors or hood of a car.

A blacksmith hammers softened metal into the shape of a horseshoe.

Metal can be rolled into long, flat sheets of many different thicknesses.

Fantastic Fact

Thin sheets of *aluminum* foil are used to wrap up food. Aluminum is one of the few metals that can be crushed into a ball.

Recycling Metal

When people buy new metal goods, they often throw the old ones away. This is a waste. Metal can be **recycled** and used to make new things. This protects our **environment**.

Why Recycle?

Getting rid of old metal can be a problem. Metal does not burn or rot away easily. The best solution is to recycle it. Recycling metal saves the **energy** that is used to dig up, crush, and heat the ores. This cuts down on the **pollution** that comes from burning fuels.

Old, rusting metal goods can be sharp and dangerous.

24

When these old cars have been melted down, the metal will be used to make many other things.

From Scrap to Steel

Old metal goods such as refrigerators and cars can be taken to a scrapyard. The steel is melted down and used to make new things. Recycling saves the material and the energy that was used to make it.

Fantastic Fact

A baked-bean can may contain steel that was once part of a car. When the can is next recycled, it might end up in a ship or a razor.

New Cans from Old

Drinks cans are made from aluminum. Aluminum is expensive to produce and causes damage to the environment. Never throw away an aluminum can because it can easily be recycled.

What Is Aluminum?

Aluminum is a very light metal that is used to make many things. It is produced from an ore called **bauxite**. Bauxite is found in hot places such as rain forests. The bauxite is taken to a factory, where it is heated to produce aluminum.

Huge areas of rain forest are cut down in order to dig up bauxite.

Lumps of bauxite have to be heated to very high temperatures to produce aluminum. This takes a lot of energy.

Recycling Aluminum

Aluminum is used to make drinks cans, which can be recycled when they are empty. The cans are collected in can banks and crushed into *bales*.

Empty aluminum cans are collected in can banks.

At the recycling factory, the bales are heated until they melt. As the aluminum cools and begins to harden, it is rolled into new metal sheets.

This bale of crushed cans will be recycled into brand new cans.

Try This

Aluminum cans look the same as cans made of steel. Sort one from the other by using a magnet. What happens when you put the magnet near an aluminum can? What happens when you put it near a steel one?

Glossary

alloy   a metal that is made by mixing two or more metals together

aluminum   a light, silver metal that is used to make drinks cans and many other things

bale   a large bundle

bauxite   an ore than contains aluminum

conductor   a material such as metal that allows heat or electricity to pass through it easily

copper   a soft, reddish-brown metal

electricity   a kind of energy that provides people with heat, light, and the power for machines

energy   the power that makes machines and living things able to work

environment   the world around us, including the land, the air, and the sea

flexible   bendable

furnace   a very hot oven

mold	a container with a special shape
nugget	a lump of gold or other metal
ore	a rock that contains metal
platinum	a silvery-white precious metal
pollution	spoiling the air, land, or water with harmful substances
quarries	places where rocks are dug out of the ground
recycle	to make an object or material into something else
rusty	covered with a reddish-brown coating that forms on some metals when they get wet
stainless steel	a steel alloy that does not rust
steel	a very strong alloy that is made from iron

Index